EVERYDAY LIFE OF ANIMALS

LIFE CYCLES

Text by Marco Ferrari

Illustrations by Ivan Stalio

CHERRYTREE BOOKS

The series EVERYDAY LIFE OF ANIMALS was conceived and
designed by McRae Books, Florence.

Text by Marco Ferrari
Illustrations by Ivan Stalio
Consultant for UK edition Michael Chinery

Copyright © McRae Books 1997

English edition published by Cherrytree Press Ltd
Windsor Bridge Road, Bath BA2 3AX

Copyright © Cherrytree Press Ltd 1997

British Library Cataloguing in Publication Data
Ferrari, Marco
    Life cycles. – (Everyday life of animals)
    1. Animal life cycles – Juvenile literature
    I. Title
    571.8′1

ISBN 0 7451 5295 3

Colour separations by R.A.F. (Florence)
Printed in Italy

CONTENTS

INTRODUCTION

A moment during courtship

Millions of plants and animals struggle for survival every day of their lives. Each of them employs countless strategies in an effort to win the battle of life. Some depend on cunning, some on speed, some on strength or mimicry to ensure that their genes will be handed on to the next generation. A lion chasing a zebra is a classic example of what 19th-century scientists defined as 'the struggle for life'. The predator has to be faster or more cunning than its prey, while the prey depends largely on the principle of safety in numbers. But animals have invented much more subtle ways of ensuring their survival. Every strategy, every move and step made by all species can be explained only by taking into account what every individual is aiming for – reproduction. The object is to contribute as many genes as possible to later generations. Every animal and every plant has adopted a particular life style that is successful in its particular environment. Some simple life forms depend on the effective strategy of number. Bacteria, for example, simply overrun their environment with millions of tiny copies of themselves. More complex organisms produce fewer offspring as a rule, but a lot more energy goes into ensuring their survival, and this often means careful selection of mates. This is what lies behind the incredible acrobatics of the male bird of paradise as he displays his plumage to the female, or extraordinary structures such as the peacock's tail or the antlers of the stag (male deer), whose sole purpose is to convince the female that the owner is the most desirable male and get her to pair with him. And this is also what lies behind the territorial struggles, sometimes battles to the death, which become more and more ritualized as animals evolve. But it is in the care of their offspring that the highest degree of perfection in adaptation to the surrounding world has been achieved. Mammals devote a high proportion of their body resources to raising their young. Some insects even sacrifice themselves, and allow their larvae to feed on their internal organs. *Life Cycles* looks at the strategies that animals have developed, of the intricate interactions with other members of the same species and of the extraordinary solutions adopted in their struggle for survival.

LIFE STYLES

Animals appear to face many choices. Live alone or in society? Lay many eggs or only a few? Be choosy in seeking a mate or leave it to chance? Each of these alternatives involves a different life style, either rich and fascinating, or simple but effective.

Various mechanisms are involved in the making of these choices and they can be understood only when seen as part of the theory of evolution by means of natural selection, formulated in the 19th century by Charles Darwin. Every physical characteristic of an animal, said Darwin, evolved solely to allow an individual to transmit its genetic make-up to its descendants. Behaviour can be explained in the same way. The long history of the evolution of life on Earth has moulded behaviour to make possible the survival and reproduction of the species. The modern theory of evolutionary biology, which developed in the 1960s, went on to explain phenomena which formerly seemed incomprehensible, such as animal societies and the 'sacrifice' of worker bees and ants, who delegate reproduction to the queen alone.

When we say that an animal is faced with a choice, this does not mean that the decision is a conscious one, but only that millions of years of behavioural evolution have made the individual behave as if it were equipped with a sense of destiny. It is only from this point of view, of time immemorial and extremely slow changes, that we can understand how and why animals behave as they do.

GROWING A NEW LIMB OR A WHOLE NEW INDIVIDUAL FROM AN ARM
Starfish are marine invertebrates. There are about 1,800 species living in oceans throughout the world. Most starfish have five hollow arms covered with short spines and tiny pincers. If an arm gets bitten off, the starfish can grow a new one in its place. The majority of starfish reproduce by laying eggs which hatch into new individuals, but a few species of starfish reproduce by dividing their bodies into two parts. Each part becomes a new individual.

SOCIAL LIFE
The social life of many mammals, like these Thomson gazelles, is often governed by precise rules, which vary according to the season and the environment. For example, to defend themselves from predators, the gazelles gather in groups to discourage and confuse attacker by their number. But when it is time to give birth, they look for a peaceful private place.

BREAKING OUT AT BIRTH
Like most modern reptiles, crocodiles lay eggs from which their offspring hatch after a period of incubation. This young crocodile is pulling itself out of its egg. The tiny crocodile has a special horny patch on its snout to help break the egg's leathery covering.

ANIMALS THAT LOOK LIKE FLOWERS
Although they look like plants, sea anemones are animals. They attach themselves to hard surfaces, such as a rock or seashell, and seldom move. These beadlet anemones show typical aggressive behaviour as they compete for space.

PRIVATE NESTING HABITS
The female hornbill seals herself inside a cavity in a tree, rock face or earth bank when nesting. She stays there until her chicks are half-grown. All the time she relies on the male to bring food and water, which he passes through the nest-hole.

LIFE BEGINS

Animals reproduce in a variety of ways. Only a small number of species (about three per cent) give birth to live young. They are usually land animals, although whales and some fish give birth to live or active young. The majority of animals lay eggs, from which their young emerge after a period of incubation. Most animals reproduce sexually; the sperm and egg from the two parents combine to form a new individual, with a mixture of characteristics from both. A few animals, such as the sponge, can also reproduce asexually, which means that a new individual is formed from a single parent.

NESTING IN A HOLE IN THE GROUND
Many snails, including the Roman snail, dig holes in soft, damp soil where they place their eggs. They cover them with earth to keep them safe from predators until they hatch. After a few weeks, tiny, fully-formed snails emerge.

MASS SPAWNING
Coral reefs are made up of millions of tiny, soft-bodied animals, called polyps. When breeding, the polyps release bundles of eggs and sperm that float upwards and burst open. The sperm and eggs combine to produce larvae, which drift in the sea until they settle and turn into polyps themselves. Coral polyps also reproduce asexually.

LIVE BIRTHS
The Arabian oryx is a species of antelope that lives in the deserts of Arabia. Like almost all mammals, it gives birth to live young. The female oryx usually produces a single calf; multiple births are rare. The baby oryx is on its feet a few minutes after birth and can keep up with the rest of the herd within a few hours.

ASEXUAL REPRODUCTION
Until the 19th century, sponges were thought to be plants. Today, biologists class them as animals. Some sponges reproduce asexually in a process called 'budding'. This occurs when a piece of the adult animal separates and becomes a new individual. Many sponges also reproduce sexually.

THE FINAL MOULT
Cicada nymphs live underground for several years. They moult five times before emerging as fully-formed adults.

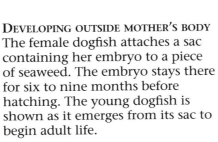

DEVELOPING OUTSIDE MOTHER'S BODY
The female dogfish attaches a sac containing her embryo to a piece of seaweed. The embryo stays there for six to nine months before hatching. The young dogfish is shown as it emerges from its sac to begin adult life.

PHASES OF GROWTH

Many plants reproduce asexually, but invertebrates are the only animals to do so. All vertebrates (mammals, fish, reptiles, birds and amphibians) reproduce sexually. Two sex cells (sperm and egg), each carrying hereditary 'instructions' typical of the species, combine in a process called fertilization. The fertilized egg is called an embryo. Fertilization and the development of the embryo can occur inside the female parent, or outside, depending on the species. The embryo develops according to the 'instructions' received and grows into a new individual of the right kind. Many animals, such as frogs, still have to go through another stage of development before they reach their adult form.

FROM EGG TO LARVA TO ADULT
Gastropods (snails and slugs) live on land, in fresh water and in the sea. Some species, like the Portuguese orange sea snail (left), lay strings of eggs in rockpools. The fertilized eggs hatch into larvae, called veligers, which can swim. The veligers drift with the currents and then sink to the bottom of a pool, where they turn into crawling snails.

A FERTILIZED EGG
The small red spot in the middle of this egg yolk is a three-day-old chicken embryo. One week later the tiny embryo will be chick-shaped.

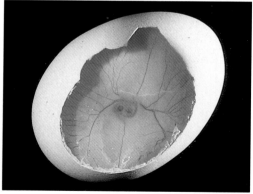

FROM EGG TO CHICKEN
After about a month the chick is fully formed and covered in soft down. It uses its beak to break the egg shell and hatches. The chick develops directly into an adult without passing through any other stage.

FROM EGG TO TADPOLE

During the breeding season, many frogs gather together in large, noisy groups. The females respond to the loud mating calls of the males. Very few frogs give birth to live young; most lay eggs in or near water. The female produces anywhere between one and 25,000 eggs, depending on the species. In most species, the eggs are fertilized outside the frog's body and are left to hatch by themselves. Only a few species protect and care for their eggs and young. Inside the egg, a tiny tadpole with a round body and long tail develops. When the tadpole hatches, it lives in the water and breathes through gills, like a fish.

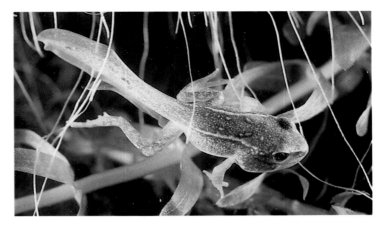

FROM TADPOLE TO FROG

Unlike adult frogs, tadpoles are mainly herbivores. They feed on algae and other underwater plants. After a period of growth, the tadpole undergoes a striking change. Its hind- and forelimbs appear and its tail gradually shrinks away. It also develops lungs, eyelids and a new digestive system to cope with a mainly carnivorous diet as an adult. This process is called metamorphosis.

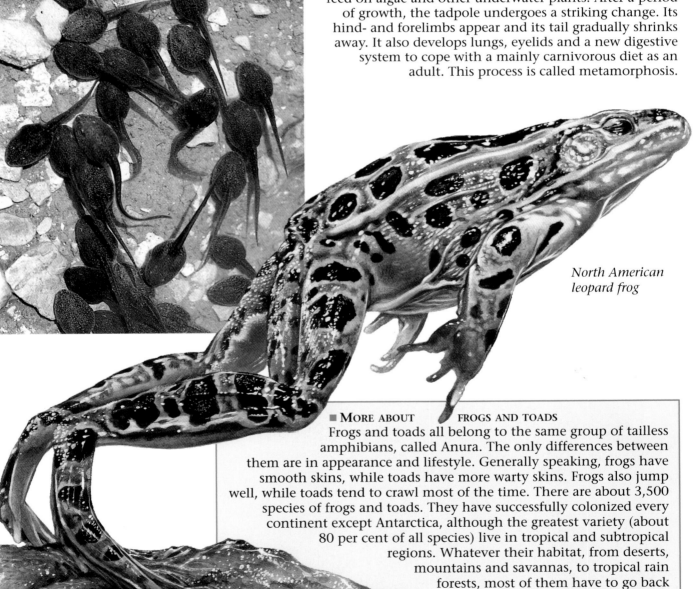

North American leopard frog

■ **MORE ABOUT** **FROGS AND TOADS**

Frogs and toads all belong to the same group of tailless amphibians, called Anura. The only differences between them are in appearance and lifestyle. Generally speaking, frogs have smooth skins, while toads have more warty skins. Frogs also jump well, while toads tend to crawl most of the time. There are about 3,500 species of frogs and toads. They have successfully colonized every continent except Antarctica, although the greatest variety (about 80 per cent of all species) live in tropical and subtropical regions. Whatever their habitat, from deserts, mountains and savannas, to tropical rain forests, most of them have to go back to the water to breed.

METAMORPHOSIS

As we have already seen, most kinds of frog go through major changes as they grow: egg – tadpole – frog. The majority of invertebrates also pass through a juvenile, or larval stage. The most striking changes occur in certain types of insects, such as butterflies and moths, beetles, flies and wasps. Their life cycles have four stages: egg – larva – pupa – adult. The larva differs greatly from the adult. It is wingless and its lifestyle is suited for growth and development rather than for reproduction. The larva often lives in a different habitat from the adult and eats different kinds of food. This ensures that members of the same species do not compete for space and food. The larva becomes a pupa and then changes to the adult form.

AMAZING INSECTS!
Of all the animals that are known, the class Insecta contains the largest number of species. More than 80 per cent of all animals are insects. And, although more than one million species of insects have been described, scientists estimate that there are at least two million more yet to be discovered.

A caterpillar hatches from its egg.

■ ABOUT BUTTERFLIES AND MOTHS
Butterflies and moths belong to a huge order of insects, called Lepidoptera. The name comes from Greek and means 'scaly winged', and it refers to the dusty scales that cover the wings, body and legs of the insects. Although they belong to the same order, moths and butterflies differ in size and life style. Most moths are nocturnal (active at night), whereas butterflies are diurnal (active during the day). Moths usually have larger bodies, smaller wings, and are less colourful than butterflies. Not only do butterflies have more brightly-coloured wings, but they also hold them vertically over their backs when resting. Moths generally fold their wings flat. There are over 100,000 species of butterflies and moths and they live in every continent except Antarctica. Almost all feed on plants. The caterpillars of some species are pests that feed on food crops. The clothes moth caterpillar even eats our clothes.

INSECTS AND EGGS
Apart from aphids and a few other forms, insects all reproduce sexually. The females usually lay eggs – many have a long tube, called an ovipositor, which they use to place their eggs where they want them. While the baby insects are inside the egg, they feed on liquid yolk. When they are fully developed the young insects hatch. Some bite their way out of the egg. Others simply grow until they burst out.

1

Metamorphosis of the swallowtail butterfly.

2. The caterpillar turns into a pupa (chrysalis), safely bound to a twig with silk.

3. The chrysalis changes into an adult butterfly, or imago, which emerges by splitting the chrysalis skin. The four-stage life cycle of a butterfly, and other insects like it, is known as complete metamorphosis.

2

1. A caterpillar has a pair of minute antennae and a cluster of tiny eyes on each side of its head. Caterpillars have no wings and up to 16 legs.

3

4. A fully-developed adult butterfly.

NESTS AND EGGS

Some animals lay their eggs in the sea or in fresh water and leave them to hatch and grow up on their own. These animals usually lay huge numbers of eggs, since many eggs and youngsters will be eaten by predators. Other parents spend a large amount of time and effort caring for their young, and usually have only a few at a time. Preparing a home, whether it be a nest or simply a well-chosen spot for egg-laying or birth, often requires planning and lengthy preparation. An ideal home needs to offer protection from the weather and from predators. Animals use many clever methods to prepare for the arrival of their young.

HEAT-REGULATED INCUBATORS

The mallee fowl of southern Australia is a member of the megapode family. The male bird spends many months of the year working on the nest. First he digs a hole and fills it with leaves and grass. Then he covers it with sandy soil to make a mound, and hollows out chambers where the female lays her eggs. The decaying vegetation below creates heat to incubate the eggs without further help from the parents. Mallee fowls are thought to mate for life. They use the same nest year after year.

■ **MORE ABOUT MEGAPODES**
Megapodes are a family of 12 species of game birds that live in rain forests, beach vegetation, and scrub in Australia, southeast Asia and on some Pacific Islands. Most species nest in mounds or holes in the ground.

FATHER TAKES CARE

The female midwife toad (left) lays a string of 20-60 eggs. After fertilizing them, the male toad winds the sticky string of eggs round his waist and hind legs. He carries the eggs around with him on land, keeping them safe from predators. After about a month, when the eggs are ready to hatch, he moves to the water, where the eggs break open and tiny tadpoles emerge.

HANGING BASKETS

The lesser-masked weaver bird builds a hanging nest using grass and twigs. The male builds the nest to attract a female. When he has finished weaving the nest he hangs beneath it, flapping his wings in an attempt to catch the attention of females. Once a female accepts the offer, she lines the inside of the nest with soft grass and feathers, and lays her eggs. The nest hanging far above the ground keeps the eggs and chicks safe from snakes and other predators.

BRIGHT COLOURS TO ATTRACT A MATE

At breeding time, the tiny male three-spined stickleback fish turns bright red and blue as he sets about building a nest and attracting a female. Using strands of water plants and secretions from his kidneys to stick them together, he builds a domed nest. When a female shows interest, he shows her the nest and, if she approves, she lays her eggs inside. The male fertilizes the eggs and protects them until they hatch. As he cares for the eggs, his skin turns to more neutral colours that will not attract predators.

PARENTS

After weeks, months or, in some cases, even years of preparation, the animal babies are finally born. During the first weeks of life the two main chores for parents are keeping their often helpless offspring safe from predators and finding enough food for them to survive. In many cases, care of the newborn animals is left almost entirely to the mother. Among mammals, the female feeds her young on milk that she produces herself. Mammal mothers usually lick their offspring clean soon after birth. The mother can then recognize her baby by its scent. Among birds, males often help their mates in feeding and caring for offspring. In only a few species, such as the sea horse, are the fathers entirely responsible for their young.

■ **MORE ABOUT THE PLATYPUS**
Almost all mammals give birth to live young. However, the duck-billed platypus of eastern Australia and Tasmania is one of three species of egg-laying mammals. (The others, called echidnas, or spiny anteaters, live in Australia and New Guinea.) The platypus spends most of its life in freshwater lakes and streams where it feeds on fish, frogs, crustaceans, molluscs, tadpoles and earthworms. It is an excellent swimmer, using its sensitive beak to find food and navigate underwater. The platypus is one of the very few mammals with venom. The male has a poison spur on the ankle of each hind foot, which it uses to fight with other males during the mating season. A jab from the spur produces enough poison to kill a dog.

AN EGG-LAYING MAMMAL
The female platypus digs a long, twisting passage in the earth with a chamber at the end. In it she lays one, two or three sticky, soft-skinned eggs about a month after mating. She curls her body round the eggs and after about ten days of incubation they hatch. The platypus suckles her young for about four months. Since she has no teats, her babies have special long lips to lap up the milk as it oozes from slits in her body. The young platypuses stay in the burrow for about three months. During that time, when the mother leaves the burrow to hunt, she plugs the entrance with soil to keep out predators, such as snakes.

KEEPING SAFE IN FATHER'S POUCH
The female sea horse lays her eggs in a special pouch on the male's abdomen (below). The male fertilizes the eggs, feeds them with a nourishing liquid that the pouch secretes, and keeps them safe from predators. After a few weeks a brood of sea horses hatches; the young are pushed out from the pouch by a series of contractions.

CARRYING WATER TO THIRSTY CHICKS
Most species of sandgrouse live in dry areas of Africa and the Middle East. Their young usually hatch in nests that are far from watering holes. For at least two months, until they are old enough to fly, the babies rely on their father to bring them drinking water. The male sandgrouse (above) flies to the watering hole, which may be 20-30 km (12-20 miles) away, and soaks his specially adapted and absorbent breast feathers in the water. He stays in the water for up to 20 minutes soaking up liquid. Then, with his precious cargo aboard, he flies back to the nest. When he returns he stands up straight and the young birds run to drink from his breast. When they have drunk their fill, he rubs his belly in the sand to dry his feathers. Although female birds are capable of carrying water, and will do so if the male dies, the job is generally done by males. By dividing the work of caring for their young, the parents are more likely to be able to raise their brood to adulthood.

MAKING CONTACT AFTER BIRTH
The female bison of North America carries her single calf in the womb for about nine months. After this period of gestation, she often leaves the herd to give birth, rejoining it as soon as her calf is strong enough to stand. Immediately after birth, she licks her baby clean, freeing its nostrils so it can breathe and drying its fur so that its body holds in heat. This act of motherly care establishes a bond that lasts for about four years.

EARLY DAYS

As the young animals grow, their parents spend time and energy protecting them from predators. Even normally calm parents, especially females, become aggressive and will sometimes place themselves in danger when defending their offspring. Many mothers carry their young on their backs during the first weeks or months of life. This allows them to move more quickly than they could if the young were following on their own. It also saves the babies precious energy needed for growth. In higher animals, particularly mammals, affectionate and long-lasting relationships are established.

HITCHING A RIDE
When danger threatens, female swans ferry their brood out of harm's way. The cygnets nestle into the feathers on their mother's back. Swans can be very aggressive when defending their young.

■ MORE ABOUT SCORPIONS
There are over 1,200 species of scorpion. They all have long, venomous tail stings and five pairs of legs including the big pincers. Scorpions are mainly nocturnal and feed on spiders and insects. They use the front pair of pincers for grasping prey and tearing it apart. During courtship, scorpions perform a ritual dance during which the male fertilizes the female. Males that stay near females after mating are sometimes killed and eaten by them. The fertilized eggs develop inside the female and, several months after mating, live young are born. A typical litter has about 25 young scorpions.

IN THE SHELTER OF A LETHAL STING
Newborn scorpions crawl onto their mother's back where they are protected from predators by her sting. They stay on her back for up to six weeks. During that time they absorb water through the female's skin and use food reserves built up before birth. If the female scorpion is unable to spend a lot of time caring for her young, they will not survive.

TAKING CARE OF BABY
Chimpanzees are social animals that live in small bands, usually based on family relationships. These small bands often group together in communities of up to 100 individuals. Female chimpanzees can give birth at any time of year to a single baby (or, more rarely, twins) after eight to nine months in the womb. Mother chimpanzees nurse their young for as long as two or three years. During this time, very strong relationships develop between the mother and her offspring. This special relationship appears to last forever, even after the birth of other offspring. If a female dies while caring for a young chimpanzee, its older brothers and sisters will often take care of it. Chimpanzees use a wide range of sounds and facial expressions. They often kiss, hug, embrace and groom one another, seeming to show affection for other group members.

A female chimpanzee carefully removes something from her baby's eye.

BUILDING FAMILY BONDS
After a gestation period of about three months, female cheetahs give birth to two to four cubs. As the cubs are born blind and helpless, the mother cheetah takes care to give birth in thick scrub or dense bush where her cubs will be safe from predators. Juveniles have a thick mane on their neck and shoulders, which acts as camouflage. It makes them look larger and fiercer than they actually are, and gives the mother something to grip when carrying them by the scruff of the neck. Cheetahs suckle their young for about three months, although by six weeks the cubs are big enough to start learning how to hunt. Like all members of the cat family, cheetahs keep very clean. The mother cheetah spends time grooming her cubs. They are independent by about 18 months of age.

FIRST FOOD

A plentiful supply of high-quality food is essential during the early stages of an animal's life. Protein, vitamins, sugars and fats are needed to help the young animal develop and grow. Where parents are not involved in caring for their young, they often lay their eggs on or near a rich food source so that their offspring will have food when they hatch. Mammal babies are among the most fortunate of young animals because their mothers suckle them on milk until they can feed themselves. During the first few days after birth, the mother's milk also contains antibodies to protect the baby from infection. Bird parents are kept busy for weeks after their chicks hatch.

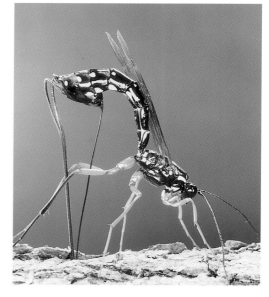

PREPARING MEALS IN ADVANCE
Many insects lay their eggs directly on or in food sources so that when the larvae hatch they will have a ready supply of food. The larva of this ichneumon wasp feeds on the larvae of wood wasps found in pine trees. The female ichneumon wasp searches the bark of trees until she detects a larva underneath. Using a long, specially adapted tube, she bores a hole in the tree and places an egg on top of the wood wasp larva. When the ichneumon wasp larva hatches, it eats the larva of the wood wasp before turning into a pupa. The pupa develops in the safety of the tree until it becomes an adult wasp the following year.

TAP THE RED SPOT ON MOTHER'S BEAK
Like most species of gull, herring gulls mate for life. In early summer the birds come together to nest in colonies on cliff ledges or coastal islands. After mating, the female lays two or three eggs. Parents share the task of incubating the eggs, changing over every few hours. When the chicks hatch, they instinctively peck at the red spot on their parent's bill. This makes her regurgitate the food she has in her crop. The chicks stay close to the nest for about a week. Their parents protect them from other adults, which sometimes prey on their neighbours' young.

'CROP MILK' FOR FLAMINGO CHICKS
Some groups of birds, including flamingos and pigeons, feed their young on 'milk'. Since flamingos usually nest far from food sources, they solve the problem of carrying food back to their young by regurgitating a kind of 'milk' or 'soup' made from food they have swallowed themselves, called crop milk. Both male and female birds produce crop milk. Studies have shown that even flamingos that are not parents care for orphan chicks in this way. The persistent begging calls of the hungry youngsters seem to stimulate the production of a hormone that allows the birds to produce milk.

AQUATIC MAMMAL BABIES
A Galapagos sea lion mother suckles her pup. Aquatic mammals, including whales, dolphins, seals and walruses, all feed their young on milk, just as their land-lubber cousins do.

A flamingo parent feeding its chick on crop milk. The baby birds lose their fluffy down at about 12 weeks. It takes several years for their grey juvenile colour to change to adult pink.

■ MORE ABOUT FLAMINGOS

Flamingos are strange-looking birds, with long thin legs and necks, small heads and huge, curved beaks. They have large bodies, and white or pink feathers, depending on the species. Males are 80-145 cm (31-57 in) tall, while females are slightly shorter. There are several species and they range over southern South America, Africa, southern Europe, and the Middle East. They are social birds and stay together in flocks. At mating time they come together in huge colonies. An estimated two million birds gather in a single colony around Lake Nakuru in the Rift Valley, Kenya. Flamingos mate for life, and both parents help to build the nest of mud, where the female lays a single egg. The parents take turns at incubating the egg until it hatches and both share in the tasks of raising their offspring. Flamingos seem to live quite a long time; 50-year-old birds have been recorded in the wild. Flamingos are wading birds. When feeding, they hold their bills upside-down in the water or mud, straining it for algae, molluscs, fish and other small animals. Some species eat only microscopic organisms, while others eat much larger food.

GROWING UP

The age at which the young become capable of surviving alone varies greatly from species to species. A few days or even less may be sufficient for many fish and reptiles, while most insects and other invertebrates are independent as soon as they are born. Most of the abilities for survival are inbuilt, and the offspring have little to learn from their parents. They are able to find food for themselves immediately. But if the baby has to develop complex skills, such as learning how to hunt, for example, or how to move around in the forest canopy and not fall from trees, then it is dependent on its parents for much longer. The animals that take the longest to become independent are those with the largest brains, such as birds or mammals.

ORANGUTAN
The offspring of the orangutan, an ape that lives on various islands of southeast Asia, stay with their mother for a long time because they have to learn how to choose the right fruit and leaves to eat, and how to move around the forest. The youngsters also learn to build temporary shelters in the trees, where they can rest at night. The newborn babies are able only to hold on to their mother's fur for protection, especially from male members of the group. The males are dangerous, as they are always looking for females to mate with, and will chase away the baby if it is in the way.

KANGAROO
Marsupials, or pouched animals, like this small kangaroo, have developed a unique method of looking after their babies. The neonate, or undeveloped baby, slowly moves from the uterus to the mother's pouch, where it latches on to her teat. Not until many weeks later is the baby kangaroo ready to leave the pouch for the first time. It follows its mother as she moves around in search of fresh grass to eat.

INDIAN ELEPHANT
Within elephant herds, both Indian and African, different kinds of social behaviour are found, both friendly and aggressive. This is why elephant calves can take up to six or seven years to grow up. They only become adult members of the group once they have learned all the rules of elephant behaviour. They stay with their mother until they are fully grown.

GOLDEN EAGLE
Eagles, and many other birds of prey, generally lay two eggs at different times. The second chick to hatch is much smaller than the older chick. Often the older chick bullies or even kills the second chick. Once the competitor has been eliminated, the parents can devote themselves to feeding the remaining chick and ensuring that it survives and learns to hunt.

■ **MORE ABOUT GOLDEN EAGLES**
Golden eagles start to breed when they are about four years old and keep the same mate for life. Each pair guards a territory and builds a nest, called an eyrie. Many golden eagles build two nests and use them in alternate years, adding new material each time. Over the years, the great shaggy nest might grow from 1 m (3 ft) across to 3 m (9·5 ft).

23

LEARNING

Many young animals are taught by their parents to hunt and find food. Like all large cats, leopard cubs go with their parents on hunting trips. By watching them hunt and by practising with their help, the cubs learn the skills they need to survive. Animals do not necessarily stop learning once they become adults. Many examples have been recorded of fully grown animals discovering ways to find food or to improve its taste – often by accident. They have repeated the method later, and even taught it to other individuals in their group so that it becomes a part of their normal behaviour.

■ MORE ABOUT MACAQUE MONKEYS
There are about 15 species of macaques, all living in Asia and North Africa. Although colour differs among the species, they are generally brown or blackish-brown. Males are larger than females, weighing 3·5-8 kg (8-17 lb). Some species live along coasts or on islands and are able to swim. They are omnivores and they all have large cheek pouches in which they carry extra food. Japanese macaques live farther north than any other monkey. During the cold winters they sometimes bathe in hot springs.

LEARNING FROM EACH OTHER
A young female Japanese macaque monkey on the Pacific island of Koshima learned that washing the sand from potatoes left by biologists made them taste better. After just a few weeks, the other monkeys in her troop began to copy her.

THE ENDLESS GAME OF LIFE

From early on in life, most young mammals play and have mock fights with their parents, and brothers and sisters. This helps them to develop control of their eyes and muscles, learning skills for defence and hunting that will be essential in adulthood. Through play, animals that live in groups also learn about the group hierarchy, or 'pecking order'.

HAVING A SMASHING TIME

Many animals have learned to use tools to find food, build homes, or frighten predators. Egyptian vultures like to eat ostrich eggs. The Egyptian vulture below is holding a stone in its beak, which it will smash down on the ostrich egg beneath. When they find eggs in sandy areas, where there are no suitable stones, the vultures sometimes fly quite long distances to pick one up.

MILK THIEVES

In Britain, where milk is still sometimes delivered to people's front doors, some tits learned to pierce the aluminium bottle tops to get at the cream. The skill spread rapidly through the country, as the tits copied each other. Biologists think that the birds learned by watching each other. The reward of a rich drop of cream was enough to encourage them to try the trick for themselves. Birds of different species have also been known to copy others' behaviour.

MALES AND FEMALES

In some animal species, one sex is much larger or more striking in appearance than the other. This is called sexual dimorphism. In many species, the males are larger, more aggressive, or more brightly coloured than the females. In other species, such as angler fish and spiders, the females are larger and more aggressive than the males. Biologists believe that these differences exist to help the species reproduce itself and survive. For example, if the female angler fish were not huge and the males were not permanently attached to her, they would have trouble finding her in the dark ocean depths where they live, and it is unlikely that they would be able to reproduce.

■ MORE ABOUT ANGLER FISH
There are over 200 species of angler fish. Most of them live on the sea bed, often in very deep waters. Many species have a long spine on their back with a coloured or luminous 'bait' on the end. By waving this about, they attract fish, which swim up close to investigate. When they are within range the angler fish swallows them.

A CLOSE RELATIONSHIP
Some female deep-sea angler fish grow up to 20 times the size of the males. The male fish have pincer-like teeth, and during the breeding season they bite into a female's skin and fertilize her eggs as she lays them. The males stay attached to her for the rest of their lives. The male is totally dependent on the female for food and oxygen; gradually even his blood fuses with hers. Sometimes two or more males attach themselves to the same female.

A CAUTIOUS APPROACH
When a male spider wants to mate, he must take great care to identify himself when approaching a female and make a quick escape afterwards. Many females are larger than the males and, if they mistake the male for prey, they may eat him. The eggs are laid in a silk sac that the female carries around with her or hides until the eggs hatch.

SIAMESE FIGHTING FISH
Siamese fighting fish have traditionally been kept and bred for use in fighting contests. The specially-bred fish are very brightly coloured with long fins. The males are very aggressive; during courtship and mating, they bite and batter the females in a frenzied whirl of colour. To attract the attention of the females, the male fish can brighten or even change their colours.

MAMMAL MALES
Sexual dimorphism is common in mammals. Males are often larger and more powerful than females. This is because the males fight among themselves; the biggest and strongest are the most successful and they pass these characteristics on to their offspring. Females most often mate with males that are in some way 'superior' to the others. So, the larger and more powerful males mate more often, and their characteristics are reproduced. The male sheep, or ram, is in the middle of this picture.

RIVALRY

Animals not only have to defend themselves from predators of other species, but also often have to struggle with members of their own species. During courtship and mating, males fight to gain or keep control of females or mating grounds. Territorial animals defend their territory from others throughout the year. Social or herding animals often fight to establish or preserve their position within the group hierarchy. Young animals in a litter or clutch where food and warmth are scarce also compete with each other. Competition between sisters and brothers is called sibling rivalry.

KANGAROO BOXING
Kangaroos live in Australia and New Guinea. The largest species, with males standing over 2 m (7 ft) tall, travel in mobs led by a dominant male called the 'old man' or 'boomer'. He dominates younger rivals by biting, kicking and boxing.

INSECTS IN COMBAT
Sexual dimorphism, where males and females are quite different from each other is common in insects. Among stag beetles, the males have greatly enlarged mandibles (jaws). They look like the antlers of a stag, hence the name of the species. The males use their huge jaws to wrestle with other males to compete for females. Rival stag beetles interlock their jaws in much the same way as stags do their antlers.

SIBLING RIVALRY AMONG BIRDS
When food is scarce or the number of offspring is particularly large, brothers and sisters compete with each other for food. Among birds, the noisiest hatchlings with the largest gape attract their parents' attention and receive the most food. Weaker nestlings often die, but at least some of the others survive.

■ **MORE ABOUT KOMODO DRAGONS**
Komodo dragons are the largest lizards in the world. They grow up to 3 m (10 ft) long and weigh about 135 kg (300 lb). They are part of the monitor lizard family and live on Komodo Island and neighbouring islands in Indonesia. The animals live in deep burrows where they lay eggs that hatch in April and May. The hatchlings live in trees during the first months of their lives. Although they feed mainly on carrion (dead animals), adult komodo dragons have been known to attack and kill members of their own species, as well as larger mammals, including humans.

A FEARSOME DISPLAY
Lizards often use threatening displays, including colour changes, body inflation, push-ups, tail waving and head movements, to warn individuals of their own species or others to keep off their territory or away from a mate. Many males, like these komodo dragons, gain territory at the beginning of the mating season and defend it from others in ferocious battles.

COMMUNICATION

Animals use a variety of signs and signals to communicate information to others. Some of the most common signals include: marking a territory with scent; showing a flash of colour in defence or warning; singing or calling during courtship and mating, or to stay in touch; body language for defence or for pulling rank.

SONG OF THE HUMPBACK WHALE
Whales have extremely good hearing. They can hear sounds – called 'phonations' – that are far too high- or low-pitched for humans to hear. They can also tell from which direction sounds come. Humpback whales make a wide variety of sounds, strung together in a sequence that forms a 'song' that lasts between 7 and 10 minutes and is then repeated. All the whales sing the same basic song, which they can hear from as far as 80 km (50 miles) away. So far scientists have been unable to find out what the songs mean, though they have discovered that the songs change as the whales mature and grow old.

■ MORE ABOUT HUMPBACKS
The humpback whale is one of the largest whales. It is a baleen whale. Baleen is horny material that hangs in sheets like vertical blinds in the whale's mouth. These act as strainers to keep in the plankton and small fish that the whale takes in with every mouthful of water. Like many other whales, humpbacks graze in groups, or pods, of 20 or more animals. One of the most striking aspects of the humpback is its extremely long white flippers, which it sometimes raises above the surface of the water. Humpback whales are also known for the long distances they travel, from the Arctic Circle to the warm waters of the tropics, where they mate and give birth to their young.

MAY THE LOUDEST VOICE WIN

In the rutting season each spring, stags hold roaring contests to compete for the possession of harems of up to 20 females. The males' voice boxes become enlarged during the rut. The loud, roaring bellows are an invitation to fight, although few animals ever come to blows and most contests are settled by roaring alone. Roaring is an exhausting business; each stag gives out an average of five bellows per minute. The loudest animal wins, usually without a fight.

LEARNING HUMAN LANGUAGE

Attempts to teach chimpanzees to speak have failed because they do not have the right voice boxes. Chimps taught to use sign language have learned to make short sentences (eg 'Give me apple') and to recognize and express some concepts, such as 'same' and 'different'. Their language skills are at a similar level to those of a two- to three-year-old child.

BODY LANGUAGE

Animals can express a wide range of emotions through the positions of parts of the body. Wolves communicate within the pack by the position of the tail and ears. Only the leader of the pack can keep his tail raised, for example, while all the others must keep their tails 'humbly' lowered. When an animal wants to attack, he flattens his ears. This is how the wolf shows the others what it intends to do.

SONGS AND CROAKS

The animal world is almost never silent; even in the depths of night, or in the middle of a desert, the calls of birds or cries of other animals can be heard. Most animals communicate using sound, because sound can cover large distances in a short space of time. Animals use sound to attract members of the opposite sex, to keep away those of the same sex, to inform of their presence, or to give warning. They produce sound in many different ways. Some insects, such as crickets and grasshoppers, make sounds by rubbing their wings and legs together; amphibians and mammals vibrate the vocal cords in their throats. Birds have a vocal organ near their lungs, called a syrinx. The syrinx contains many membranes that vibrate, so birds can produce a variety of different sounds.

FROG TALK
Frogs and toads are among the most skilled 'singing' animals. Despite their small size, the males can make very loud croaking noises. Most of them have large 'vocal sacs' beneath their throats, which make their croaks louder. The calls of the males can usually be heard in the brief mating season when they are used to attract females and keep away other males. Animals that prey on frogs know this too. Guided by the sound of the 'spring peepers', they lose no time in hurrying to the swamps where the 'singers' are performing, to swallow them whole.

■ MORE ABOUT AMPHIBIANS

Around 370 million years ago, the amphibians were the first vertebrates to live on land. Around 4,000 species live on land today. There are tailless amphibians, such as frogs and toads, those with tails, such as salamanders and newts, and a few species of strange limbless amphibians, called caecilians. Most amphibians live on insects and other small invertebrates they catch on the ground. All of them lay their eggs in a very humid environment, or in water.

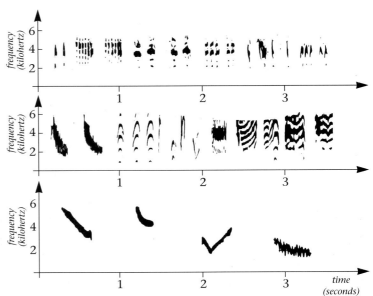

DIAGRAMS OF BIRD SONGS
Every bird has its own special song, which specialists study with highly sophisticated instruments. Above are some sonograms, which are diagrams of the songs of various species. They show the number of sounds made over a certain period of time. It has been shown that in some species the final song has to be learned from the parents, while other birds are born with all the song inbuilt in the brain.

GREAT REED WARBLER
Like many of the perching birds, the male great reed warbler sings in spring to inform others of his presence. After he has marked out his territory and provided a quiet place for the female to lay her eggs, the male alights on a high cane and begins singing his shrill song. The song of the great reed warbler is one of the most characteristic sounds of the dense European marshes.

PARROTS
Parrots (below) are among the most talkative in the world of birds. They can even do fairly good imitations of the human voice; often they sat complete phrases. Mynah birds from Asia are even better mimics than parrots. Some succeed in learning more than 700 words, though they do not know their meaning.

RELATIONSHIPS

The basis of every group of animals, from the family to the most complex society, is the close relationship between the young and the female. It is the female that makes what scientists call the greater 'parental investment'. She lays the eggs and, where parental care is involved, she is usually the one that protects and teaches the young. Few males take on family duties. Most are interested only in mating as often as possible. Only when the offspring are unable to survive alone, for example because they need to learn to hunt or have to be fed with food that is hard to find, does the male lend a hand in raising them. Larger groups such as wolf packs, lion prides and monkey societies may then be formed, each with its own complex rules of social behaviour.

THE GREAT ANTLERS OF THE MALE

Among the elks, and all other members of the deer family, it is the female that raises the young by herself. The male spends his time defending his territory, and seeks females to mate with in that area. Elks have enormous antlers for the sole purpose of fighting. The rutting season is in autumn. Young males use their antlers to challenge older males, and also to shake trees and bushes to show other elks how strong they are. Elk pairs do not stay together very long. The dominant male follows a female and keeps away other males until they have mated. Once they have mated, the pair splits up.

■ MORE ABOUT HERONS

The heron family consists of around 60 species. They live in all kinds of habitats around the world, except in the polar regions. Their long beaks and slender legs enable them to ambush their prey. Herons, egrets, and the black-crowned night heron wait patiently at the water's edge for fish, amphibians or small mammals to come within reach of their stabbing beaks. Herons vary in colour from the great white heron to the black African and Australian egrets, with a range of red, green or brown plumage in between. A small group of herons, the bitterns, are well camouflaged against the thick reeds, where they build their nests. Most other herons nest close to each other in large colonies called heronries. Colonies are often mixed, with storks, spoonbills and ibises sharing the space.

COMPLEX SOCIETIES

Baboons are monkeys that live in Africa and Arabia. Each group is an extended family, with a dominant male and a harem of females arranged in a hierarchy – order of dominance. But as in human groups, baboon society changes all the time. The dominant male can be ousted by a younger male from another group, or the highest-ranking female can lose her place because of illness or fights. This is why young baboons have to learn their place in the group.

NESTS IN TREES

Herons and egrets often build their nests in trees to keep the eggs and chicks safe from predators. Despite the fact that they live side by side in a heronry, egrets are anything but friendly to their neighbours. A number of small territories are created within the heronry, off limits to other members of the colony. If an adventurous chick leaves its nest, it is chased away and sometimes killed by its neighbours.

NOBODY BUT MUM

A bear family is very simple. It consists of the mother and her young. After mating, the male bear leaves the female to take care of the offspring by herself. The male becomes a complete stranger, and may even be a danger to the cubs. Bears are predators, and in the eyes of a male, a cub represents a chance to fill his stomach. The female must therefore not only be on the lookout for flooding rivers, wolves or hunters, but also keep an eye on the males of her own species. The cubs stay with their mother for about three years.

FEMALES TOGETHER

Both harems and matriarchies are groups of female animals living together. The difference between the two lies in the leadership. In harems, there is a dominant male, or group of males, to protect and control the females. Only the dominant male is allowed to mate with the females in the harem. Harems are common among mammals. Some harems are permanent, while others last only for the mating season. A matriarchy is a group of females led by a dominant female. Males are allowed to enter the group only during the breeding season. They are sent away soon after mating. The females in a matriarchy care for and bring up their young together.

ELEPHANT SOCIETY
Family herds of elephants are led by a dominant grandmother elephant or 'matriarch'. The herd she leads normally consists of her sisters, daughters, female cousins and all their various offspring. As group leader, the matriarch is responsible for finding sufficient food and water, and for keeping the herd safe from predators and natural dangers. If, for example, a river must be forded, the matriarch will go first, finding the best route for the crossing. Within the herd, female elephants usually have their babies at about the same time. It is quite common for sister elephants, or mothers and daughters, to help each other out by providing a babysitting service when a mother elephant needs a rest or wants to feed away from her baby.

STAG WITH HAREM
During the rut, stags become highly aggressive, fighting it out among themselves to gain control over the largest number of females. When mating is over, the harems split up. The adult males go off and form their own herds. The females and their young form separate herds, each with its own leaders. They remain in these groups until the following rut.

SEA LION HAREMS
Male sea lions are much larger than the females. During the breeding season, dominant males gather together up to 50 females in harems. The males fight one another to win control over a piece of shoreline where the females will come ashore. When the females arrive at the breeding grounds, they give birth to a single pup conceived the year before and then mate again. They mate with the male that controls their area of shoreline.

■ MORE ABOUT COATIS
Coatis live in forests and scrublands in Central and South America. They are quite closely related to raccoons. Coatis have long, upturned snouts, which they use to probe for prey. They feed on insects and other invertebrates, birds, eggs, fruit and small mammals. The males are solitary animals; they only join the female group for mating. Females build platforms in trees where they give birth to three to five babies.

CO-OPERATIVE COATI GROUPS
Female coatis live together in co-operative groups of between 5 and 12 individuals. They share guard duties, engage in mutual grooming and help each other bring up their young.

HIERARCHIES

The life of a pack, a family, or any animal society needs order. Each member of the group has to know precisely what its tasks, duties and rights are. This is why hierarchies are formed within the pack. One male or female with special characteristics always emerges the winner from battles between the various members. The strongest, cleverest or most trustworthy takes command of the group, and keeps control over the other animals. The dominant figure often looks different from the other members of the group: it may be larger or more colourful. It also behaves differently, deciding what to do at critical moments in the life of the pack.

FIGHTING FOR A MATE

Among horses, a single stallion dominates the herd, which is made up of females and colts. When still quite small, colts start to play at fighting, kicking each other and rearing up on their hind legs. They are learning behaviour that will be useful in adult life, and establishing a hierarchy. In the mating season, the stallion mates with all the females. He controls the herd until he is challenged and beaten by a younger male from a herd of 'bachelors'. Although he dominates his herd, a stallion does not have a true territory, just an area where grass and water are plentiful and through which other horses often pass. This social system is fairly rare in mammals; it is only otherwise found in two species of zebra, the plains zebra and mountain zebra, and a few other African species, such as the giant pig and the gelada baboon.

THE DOMINANT GRIFFON
A temporary hierarchy is created among griffon vultures every time they feed. When the griffons fling themselves on a carcass, the hungriest are the most aggressive. With open wings and extended claws, they try to chase away other birds landing on the meat. When they have eaten their fill, they become less aggressive and other griffons take their place. This happens every time a vulture sights carrion. But if there are different species of vulture present, the largest ones dominate, and always eat first.

THE COLOURS OF THE DOMINANT MALE
The social systems of gelada baboons and mandrills are as different as the brilliant colours that distinguish them. Gelada baboons (below), for example, live in large colonies, usually of 50-250 animals, made up of small harems belonging to an individual male, and groups of bachelor males. The harem is formed when a bachelor male succeeds in attracting one or more young females. Even though the males are dominant, it is the older and more experienced females who lead the group. Mandrills (right) live in the tropical forests of western Africa, and move in groups of about 20 animals under the command of a male. The lionlike mane of the male gelada and the blue and red cheeks of male mandrills are displayed to show other members of the group when they want to mate, attack or make peace.

LONERS

The males and females of most animal species live by themselves for most of the year. They meet with others of their species only for a brief period during courtship and mating. They return to their solitary lives as soon as mating is over. When the offspring are born, or the eggs are laid, the female either abandons them or takes care of them and brings them up on her own. In only a few cases, for example among sea horses, do the males bring up the young.

LONE GROUPERS
Despite their name, groupers are solitary fish. They are large and heavy-bodied, with big mouths. Some species can grow to 2 m (6 ft) in length and weigh up to 225 kg (500 lb). They live in warm waters throughout the world. Groupers tend to live in one place from which they hunt for prey. They are ferocious hunters. By being able to change their colour quickly to match their surroundings, they can approach their prey unseen.

LONE AMPHIBIANS
Most salamanders live in temperate regions of the northern hemisphere. They live on land or in the water, or spend a part of their time on land and a part in the water, depending on the species. Salamanders meet up at mating time and, after a brief courtship, mating takes place. In the more primitive salamanders, fertilization takes place outside the body. Among more highly evolved species, courtship is more elaborate and fertilization occurs inside the female's body. The eggs are normally laid soon after mating, but sometimes the sperm is stored and egg-laying delayed.

A SOLITARY OLD AGE

North American bison are normally social animals. They were once very numerous in North America (an estimated 50 million inhabited the Great Plains when Europeans arrived) and lived together in large herds. Numbers are now much reduced and surviving animals live in herds of 20 to 40 individuals during most of their lives. However, in old age, they often wander off on their own, leaving the herd in preparation for death.

LONE HUNTERS

The lynx is a short-tailed member of the cat family. It lives in the forests of Europe, Asia and northern North America. Most lynxes live alone in established territories, which they leave only during the mating season. During courtship, males make high-pitched wailing sounds, which females answer by howling. A litter of two or three kittens is raised by the mother. They stay with her until the next mating season, when they are chased away by new suitors.

THE SECRETIVE OCTOPUS

Octopuses are shy, secretive animals. They usually live by themselves in holes or crevices on the rocky sea bed. At breeding time, one of the male's eight tentacles develops special adaptations. At first he uses it to caress his mate, then he reaches inside his body and takes out packages of sperm, which he pushes into the female's body through her breathing tube.

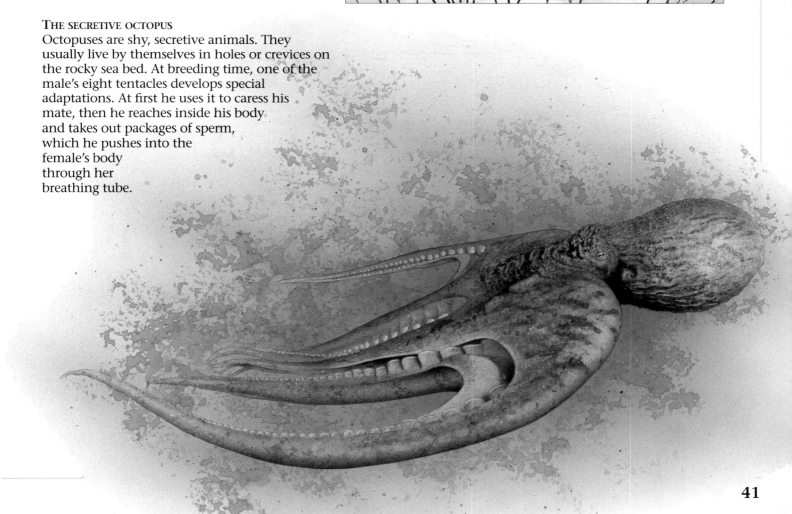

TERRITORY

CONCERTS IN THE JUNGLE
Howler monkeys are the largest monkeys in the South American rain forest. The males establish a vast territory, which they defend from other monkey bands by howls that can be heard as far as 5 km (3 miles) away. Each species has its own typical cry, which zoologists compare to the sound of a crowd on a football field. The howler monkey is able to make such loud cries because it has a specially adapted voice box that enlarges its neck and makes a more resonating sound.

We all feel at home in our own house. We know where to go to find things, and we can keep out people we do not want to see. For the same reasons, many animals fight to establish a territory of their own, and they keep away rivals with various signals. Sounds, flashes of light, odours, movements of feathers, pincers and claws are all used to mark a territory and defend it. There are different kinds of territories. The most common is a place where plenty of food is found. Hyenas, lions, wolves and humming birds chase away others that come too close in order to defend an area where they know they will always be able to find food. Some animals defend a reproductive territory. Sea lions, for example, and elephant seals, could certainly never catch fish on the beaches that they defend from outsiders. But the females with which the males will mate come ashore on just those stretches of beach. Frogs and many species of fish also establish their own reproductive territories.

SMALL UNDERWATER TERRITORIES
Many species of fish also defend a territory. Most territorial fish, like the peacock blenny, live in shallow coastal waters. The peacock blenny inhabits the rocky shorelines of the Mediterranean Sea. The male claims a small area of rocks and seaweeds, and strongly defends it from other fish. He persuades females to lay their eggs in his territory. Knowing the area well means that the blenny can escape or hide from danger when necessary.

A QUIET LIFE

Sloths, which live in the tropical forests of Central and South America, are the last survivors of a long line of once-common herbivores. These animals leave their tree only when they have to move to another tree or empty their bowels. When they do so, they dig a small hole in the ground at the base of the tree. It is thought that the excrement serves to fertilize the sloth's tree and at the same time keep away other sloths by its odour. Sloths move far too slowly ever to fight battles, so all they have to do to protect their territory is to mark their tree in this way.

LAIRS ON THE BEACH

Male fiddler crabs have a single huge claw that they move back and forth as though playing the violin. According to the naturalist Charles Darwin, the enlarged claw evolved through males fighting each other for possession of females. Those with the biggest claws were most successful at mating and passed the characteristic on to their offspring. The huge claw is also used to attract females to the holes in the sand where the males live. Thousands of these lairs, about 40 cm (16 in) long, sometimes cover whole beaches; the crabs shelter in them when high tide comes or danger threatens.

■ MORE ABOUT FIDDLER CRABS

Fiddler crabs live on many tropical beaches. The crabs feed on the detritus they find on the beach, in particular the thin layer of bacteria and other small organisms that cover the sand. The crab puts a ball of sand in its mouth, swallows any nutritious bits in it, and leaves the sand in neat balls around its lair. There are several species of fiddler crabs, each with a particular claw movement. When a number of different crabs live together on a beach, they divide up the territory according to the size of their mouths. Those with large mouths live on the part where the grains of sand are large, while those with small mouths live in areas of fine sand.

MATING GROUNDS

A territory used only to attract females for mating is called a lek, or mating area. A bird lek is often an area of only a few square metres. In open areas or in dense forest, it is a specific area where males go to display themselves to females and let them select the best one. Some species, such as the American sage grouse, use the lek as a stage on which to display their beauty and strength. Other species, such as the bowerbirds of New Guinea and Australia, try to impress females by creating elaborate 'gardens', quite unlike anything else in the animal kingdom. Very few mammals adopt the lek system, although male fallow deer have been known to use it under certain conditions. After mating, the task of raising the young falls to the females.

GARDENS MADE BY BIRDS
Bowerbirds live in New Guinea and Australia. At mating time, male bowerbirds try to impress females by building bowers – corridors or circles decorated with flowers, fruits and feathers, often in striking colours. The females come to inspect the 'gardens'. They decide which is the best and choose its owner as their mate. The great grey bowerbird below is building a decorated avenue. Other species make clean-swept courts, carpets of moss and fern, or decorate trees.

BATTLING FOR MATES

Topi (right) are a species of antelope. They are one of the few mammals to make use of the lek although they only do so when the topi population is particurlarly dense. Generally the males occupy relatively small territories, and groups of females, which live separately, pass through them. But when the population density is high, the territories of the males shrink in size until they are no more than mating areas, to which the males try to attract females. Similar behaviour occurs in the European fallow deer.

A STAGE SHOW IN THE PRAIRIE

The sage grouse lives in sagebrush country on the dry plains of western North America. In the mating season, the males parade themselves in tiny territories within the mating area. There is a strict hierarchy. The larger and more experienced males occupy the centre of the area, while the others take up position all round, with the lowest-ranking birds the farthest away. When the females arrive, the males begin their courtship dance: steps forward, rotation of wings, stiff tail feathers raised and white neck feathers puffed out into a frill. The females then choose a mate each. Even though, on the whole, the males at the centre of the area are chosen most often, those on the outside are not completely ignored.

KNIGHTS AND VASSALS

Ruffs are elegant wading birds that live in Europe. The dominant males, often those with the darkest ruffs, position themselves at the centre of the lek; the weaker males, with lighter or even white ruffs, stay on the outside. The dominant males try to gain favour with the females that pass through the area, showing themselves to be strong, aggressive and powerful. The weaker males attempt to mate with the females on their way to the centre. Since the females are attracted to the lek by the males with lighter ruffs, the dominant males do not mind them being there.

COURTSHIP

During courtship animals try to attract mates in many different ways. Among birds, the male peacock shows off the splendid colours of his tail feathers, while the male of the common tern offers the gift of a fish to the chosen female. Others, like the great crested grebe, perform ritual dances and exchange gifts. The male eagle calls a female with a loud, shrill cry. If she replies, these great birds of prey grip talons in mid-air, tumbling and cartwheeling across the sky.

A FISHY PROPOSAL

When the male arctic tern wants to find a mate he catches a fish and holds it in his beak until a female notices him. If she likes the fish, she will eat it. Then she waits to see how many more fish he will bring. If he turns out to be a good hunter, she will accept his mating proposal since she knows he will be a good provider for her chicks.

■ MORE ABOUT
BALD EAGLES

With a wingspan of 2 m (7 ft) or more, the bald eagle is one of the largest birds of prey. Its sharp eyesight, up to eight times more powerful than ours, is a great help in hunting. A bald eagle can see a fish swimming under the surface of the water from half a mile away. It snatches the fish from the waves while flying. Bald eagles also feed on carrion. They eat their catch or take it back to the nest to feed their young. At first the eaglets are brown all over, but by the time they are ready for courting, their head and tail feathers have turned white and bright enough to attract a mate.

THE DANCE OF THE GREBES

Great crested grebes have evolved an elaborate courtship dance. Both birds take part in the dance, which evolves over a period of weeks. They start by shaking their heads at each other. If this goes well, they move on to the next stages, which include ritual preening, wing-spreading displays, diving and the final 'weed' dance when the birds press against each other with pieces of weed in their beaks.

'LOOK AT ME!'

During courtship, the male frigate bird leans back on his tail, extends his wings, and with his beak pointing to the sky, inflates his deep-red throat sac. He also claps his bill, making attractive rattling sounds.

THE EYES HAVE IT

The male peacock's long tail, usually furled and stretched out behind on the ground, opens out into a splendid fan, designed to catch the females' attention. The more eye motifs the tail contains the more irresistible pea hens will find him. The male also raises the crest on his head and makes his brightly-coloured breast feathers shimmer.

MATING

Courtship is successful when it leads to mating. To guarantee the survival of their species, animals must ensure that their sex cells (sperm and egg) come into contact with each other so that fertilization and the conception of a new individual can take place. Mating takes place in a variety of ways. Internal fertilization is common among most land animals, including insects. External fertilization occurs among many aquatic animals.

FINDING A MATE BY SCENT

The male lion has a very sensitive nose; he can tell by sniffing the air carrying a female lion's scent whether she is ready to mate. Lionesses in a pride usually all come on heat at the same time so that all the males can mate and no fighting occurs.

MATING SERENADE

Grasshopper males 'sing' to attract a mate, by scraping their wings and legs together to produce a distinctive chirp. When a female comes along, the male climbs on to her back, grips her sides and fertilizes her eggs internally. She then puts her ovipositor into the ground and lays her eggs. She covers them and leaves them to hatch.

■ MORE ABOUT DRAGONFLIES

Dragonflies are insects that have four large, veiny wings. There are about 5,000 species throughout the world, although most live in the tropics. They are generally large, with wingspans of up to 16 cm (6 in), and brightly coloured. They have bulging compound eyes (made up of thousands of individual lenses), often covering most of their heads. Dragonflies are predatory animals; while flying, they catch smaller insects with their legs. They can fly very fast and, thanks to their great agility and exceptional eyesight, have been known to catch and eat their own weight in food in just 30 minutes. Many species are territorial, patrolling an area and preventing other dragonflies from entering or living there. Dragonflies often fly together during mating, and stay in a linked position until after the female has laid her eggs. After mating, the females lay their eggs in water. Dragonfly young, called nymphs, spend up to three years in the water. Then they clamber up the stem of a reed, and emerge from their nymphal skins as adults.

MATING UNDERWATER
Both land tortoises and marine turtles achieve internal fertilization after a brief courtship consisting of head bobbing, butting and biting.

COPULATION WHEEL
During mating, the male dragonfly grips the female by the neck, and she bends her body round to receive sperm from near the front of the male's abdomen. This strange position is called the copulation wheel.

HERMAPHRODITES
Some invertebrates, including many species of worms, snails and slugs are hermaphrodites. This means that each individual has both male and female reproductive organs. During mating they act as both males and females and both partners produce fertilized eggs.

LIVING IN GROUPS

Many animals live in groups. Some, such as gnus, gather by the thousands during migrations in search of better pastures, while vultures simply flock together in food groups when they sight prey. Other groups are more highly organized. Fish move around in large schools, making it harder for a predator to pick out a single animal to catch. Birds move in flocks: it is easier for a whole flock to chase away a predator, by attacking as a group, than it would be for a single bird. Some animals are even more highly organized. They live together in groups and all the individuals in a group have specific roles and functions. They work together and co-operate for the good of the whole society.

FAMILIES IN THE DESERT
Slender-tailed meerkats live in the deserts of southern Africa, in groups of 10 to 30 individuals, made up of several families. They shelter in a den together with ground squirrels and other species of meerkats. The families are close-knit, and the members help each other in everyday life. There is always an animal on guard, keeping one eye on the sky, to watch out for birds of prey, and the other on the ground, to spot ground-level hunters. All members of the family help in the search for food, and attack enemies that might threaten them.

THE PACK MOST TO BE FEARED
The wolf pack evolved as an effective way of capturing prey – large herbivores that are often bigger than their hunters. Each wolf has a specific task to perform in hunting. Wolves usually assemble in large packs. In areas where herbivores are scarce and the wolves have to make do with smaller prey, a pack may consist of only a few animals.

THE CAPE HUNTING DOG
Cape hunting dogs are related to wolves and dogs. They live south of the Sahara desert, in the broad savanna of eastern and southern Africa. Like wolves, Cape hunting dogs form quite large packs, and hunt gnus, gazelles and other antelopes of the savanna. They can run for many miles, chasing a gnu until the animal falls to the ground exhausted. As is the case with wolves, only one couple normally has pups. The others, which are often relatives of the dominant animal, may not reproduce, but help the mother raise her pups. For example, when the pack is out hunting, an 'aunt' may remain in the lair to look after the pups.

■ MORE ABOUT WOLVES
Until recently, wolves were among the most widespread and feared predators in temperate areas. They lived across North America from Alaska to Mexico, and throughout northern Europe and Russia. The campaign to kill them off has reduced their numbers to a few thousand animals. In some places, however, their howls can still be heard; in Yellowstone Park, United States, for example, where attempts are being made to reintroduce wolves. The wolf is a predator that feeds on almost any animal it can find in its territory, from small rodents to large herbivores, such as elks and deer, or even musk oxen. Wolves' hunting strategies vary according to the prey. Sometimes the pack roams the territory looking for field mice and rabbits; at other times long hunts for larger animals are organized. The territory of a wolf pack varies in size depending on the prey available and the number in the pack; more prey means a smaller territory. The packs communicate by howling, letting their neighbours know how large their group is and how strong. A complex network of territories possessed by the various packs is thus formed.

COLONIES

Some animals come together only at breeding time, forming extremely large colonies. The animals in the colony do not have specific tasks and the groups break up after the reproduction period. Other animals, especially less-evolved species, form complex and highly organized structures, acting together almost as if they were a single individual. They live together throughout their lives.

HOME BUILDERS
Coral polyps are simple organisms. Each individual coral polyp is only a few millimetres long, but together the polyps build huge limestone structures that vary in shape according to the species (below left). Inside, the polyps, protected from external dangers, continue to enlarge their home. Some of these coral structures are incredibly old (perhaps more than a thousand years old). These tiny creatures have succeeded in building the largest biological structure on earth, the Great Barrier Reef in Australia.

DIVISION OF LABOUR
The Portuguese man-of-war, related to jellyfish and coral, is not a single animal, but a group of small individuals called zooids. Each one of them has a precise function which it carries it out as best it can. Some zooids have a 'mouth', and they use their long tentacles to capture the little fish on which the colony feeds. Others are full of gas, and keep the entire complex afloat. The zooids that are responsible for reproduction produce sperm and eggs.

A HOST OF PENGUINS
During the long Antarctic winter, emperor penguins gather on the Antarctic ice for reproduction. There are about 30 huge colonies of these penguins, almost all on ice packs that remain stable throughout the winter. Just why they choose these sites, among the most inhospitable on Earth, may seem a mystery. In fact, the period when the young penguins need the greatest amounts of food for growth coincides with the beginning of the Antarctic spring. If they were to hatch at a milder time of year, they would need food most in the middle of winter, when their parents would not be able to find it.

A PROCESSION OF CATERPILLARS
Processionary caterpillars are best known for getting together in groups for finding food and defence. They spin large silk nests in the tops of pine trees. During the day, they stay under cover in these shelters, where they are protected from predators. By night, hundreds of caterpillars come out to look for food in long processions that can be over 10 m (30 ft) long. There is a group leader, and the others follow, one behind the other.

NESTS ON THE ROCKS
Boobies are among the most widespread marine birds. These elegant birds always make their nests in out-of-the-way sites, sometimes far from the mainland, such as on small islands off the coast. Here the birds gather in noisy colonies, where each pair builds a tiny nest. Despite the fact that they are so close to each other, the birds are quite aggressive and do not allow others in their territory, which is scarcely bigger than the nest. It is hard for predators to attack such a large, aggressive group of birds.

FLOCKING

Aggregations, or anonymous groups of animals, are the first stage in the development of animal societies. But, like everything in nature, aggregations do not happen by chance. While the individual animals may not know each other 'personally', as is the case in mammalian societies, the huge groups of birds, insects or fish have a precise defensive function. For example, very few predators succeed in penetrating the compact lines of a flock of birds; they can only do so if they can single out one bird. It is difficult to penetrate the flock because the predator's sight is confused by so many wings in movement. An animal group

Many fish, especially vulnerable ones such as these tropical jacks, form schools. Some fish, including sardines, remain in schools throughout their lives. They are often made up of millions of fish that swim in formation, followed by their predators, both human and animal. Aggregations of this type are anonymous groups, and the behaviour of the animals is probably hereditary, even though a certain amount of the behaviour must be learned in the first stages of life.

can be formed for different reasons. The individual members may seek each other out when food is needed or when it is time to migrate. Other animals stay together in a group from birth. The success of these strategies is shown by schools of fish, flocks of birds and of migrating locusts.

A REAL CALAMITY
For the farmers of southern Africa, the red-beaked quelea is a real problem. These small, rather dowdy-looking perching birds appear in the fields without warning and can devastate crops. They assemble in flocks of thousands or millions to forage for food, usually seeds. Predators have no chance of singling out one bird, and must wait until the flock stops to drink or nest. The trees on which they nest have to be enormous, for these small, sparrowlike birds build as many as 500 nests per tree.

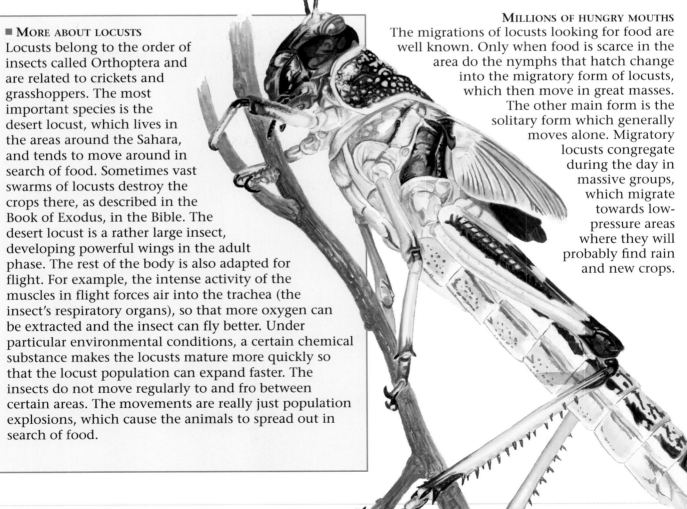

■ MORE ABOUT LOCUSTS

Locusts belong to the order of insects called Orthoptera and are related to crickets and grasshoppers. The most important species is the desert locust, which lives in the areas around the Sahara, and tends to move around in search of food. Sometimes vast swarms of locusts destroy the crops there, as described in the Book of Exodus, in the Bible. The desert locust is a rather large insect, developing powerful wings in the adult phase. The rest of the body is also adapted for flight. For example, the intense activity of the muscles in flight forces air into the trachea (the insect's respiratory organs), so that more oxygen can be extracted and the insect can fly better. Under particular environmental conditions, a certain chemical substance makes the locusts mature more quickly so that the locust population can expand faster. The insects do not move regularly to and fro between certain areas. The movements are really just population explosions, which cause the animals to spread out in search of food.

MILLIONS OF HUNGRY MOUTHS

The migrations of locusts looking for food are well known. Only when food is scarce in the area do the nymphs that hatch change into the migratory form of locusts, which then move in great masses. The other main form is the solitary form which generally moves alone. Migratory locusts congregate during the day in massive groups, which migrate towards low-pressure areas where they will probably find rain and new crops.

SOCIETIES

Social organization is the highest level an animal species can achieve. Only a few species can be called truly social animals. Apart from humans, these include bees, wasps, ants and termites, and among mammals only chimpanzees and gorillas, and an African rodent that lives underground, called the naked mole rat. Other species instead form simpler organizations, which work just as well in coping with the problems posed by the environment as complex societies. The presence of insect societies in so many ecosystems shows how successful social organization is. Bees, ants and termites have a rigidly structured society, in which the sterile workers labour for the good of the colony without reproducing.

■ **MORE ABOUT BEES**
Of all the insects on Earth, those that have been most successful are bees and ants. Bees belong to the order Hymenoptera. Bumblebee colonies, or societies, last for just one year, but the honeybee lives in permanent colonies. Since they 'learned' how to live through the winter, bees have been able to create ever larger colonies. 'Ruled' by a queen, colonies may contain as many as 80,000 individuals. Unlike termites, honeybees do not divide tasks up according to caste; all the worker bees participate in the work of the hive, changing jobs as they get older. The queen mates only once in her life with the males, or drones, which are then chased away by the workers.

ONLY EGGS FOR THE QUEEN

Termites, unlike bees and ants, belong to the order Isoptera. It is thought that termite society developed so that a secretion vital to the survival of termites could be passed from one generation to the next. With the generations living together for several years, a highly complex social life developed. Termites, like some ants, are divided into castes: there are workers, soldiers and a reproductive couple, the king and queen. The queen has an enormously enlarged abdomen and continuously produces eggs. In tropical countries, termites dominate life on the savanna; they represent a large proportion of the animals in any given area, and even alter the landscape by building mounds.

A SMALL COMMUNITY

When population density is high among rabbits, they dig a system of burrows in which about 20 adults live together. The dominant male and female live at the centre of the colony, the place best protected from predators. The offspring of the dominant couple also tend to have a high social status, and therefore remain in the centre of the colony. All the couples defend an area around their den, but there are also areas of common pasture. The subordinates live at the edge of the colony.

A SOCIETY OF WEAVERS

The sociable weaver bird is one of the most common birds in southern Africa. The weavers build enormous nests, in which up to 300 birds can live. The nests are giant piles of grass and straw, placed on trees, telephone poles or platforms. Each couple builds a nest inside the mass of grass, and continues to bring fresh straw throughout the year. The birds shelter there at night and during the hottest part of the day. The nests of the sociable weavers are also used by many other species, such as the African pygmy falcon and the grey acacia tit.

CO-OPERATION

Some animals, such as sperm whales, will help other species when they are in danger, even if this means risking their lives. Other animals establish co-operative relationships with members of different species. If both species benefit from the relationship, this is called symbiosis (meaning 'life together'). Animals mainly co-operate in keeping each other clean, providing food, or protecting each other from predators.

HELPING OUT

Sperm whales protect the members of their group. If a whale is injured the others gather round, their heads towards the middle, forming a circle known as the 'marguerite flower'. This behaviour is disastrous for the whales when they are being hunted because it allows whalers to pick them off one by one.

■ MORE ABOUT SPERM WHALES

The sperm whale has an enormous square head, taking up about one-third of its body length, and a small, underslung lower jaw. It lives in herds of 15-20 individuals. Female and juvenile whales live in temperate and tropical seas throughout the world, while lone males also venture into colder polar waters. Males grow up to about 18 m (60 ft) long; females are usually much smaller. Sperm whales are the largest of the toothed whales. They feed mainly on marine molluscs, such as cuttlefish, squid and octopus. Sperm whales dive deeper than any other aquatic mammal; they have been recorded at 1,200 m (3,900 ft) below the water surface. They have been hunted extensively for waxy substances in their bodies called spermaceti and ambergris, which are used to make cosmetics, perfumes and ointments. Moby Dick, the most famous whale in literature and leading character in Herman Melville's novel, was a sperm whale.

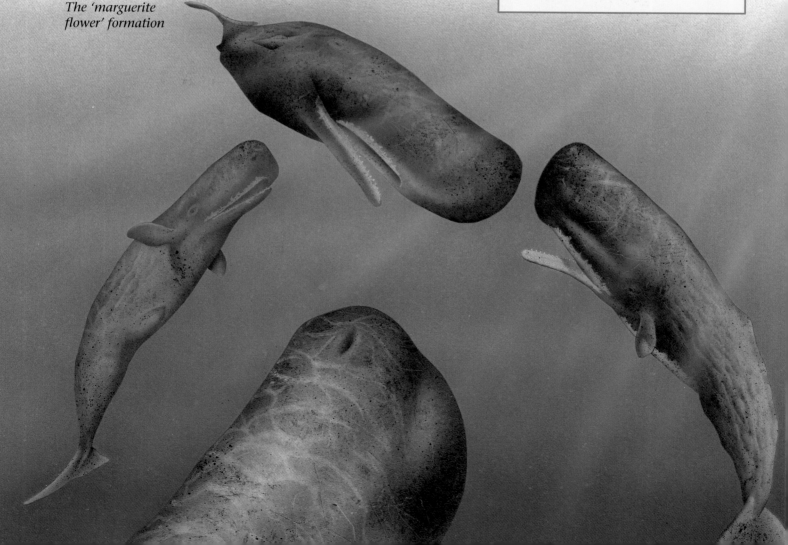

The 'marguerite flower' formation

STICKING TOGETHER
Remoras, or shark suckers, have a sucker on the top of the head with which to attach themselves to sharks, turtles and other large marine animals. The remoras do not harm their hosts; they feed on small parasites on the animal's skin, helping to keep it clean. In return, the remoras are kept safe from predators and also get a banquet meal when the shark kills large prey.

**CLEANING SERVICES
IN EXCHANGE FOR FREE MEALS**
Almost 2,500 years ago the Ancient Greek historian Herodotus noticed that while all the other animals were afraid of the crocodile and kept a respectful distance from its gaping jaws, the tiny Egyptian plover roamed freely over its body and even fluttered about inside its huge mouth. He was the first to suggest that the bird was feeding on parasites on the reptile's skin and the remains of food left in its mouth. Modern naturalists have confirmed this symbiotic relationship. As well as helping the crocodile by removing parasites, the plover acts as a 'watchdog', flying away at the approach of larger animals, though the crocodile does not really have any natural enemies.

DAIRY FARMER ANTS
Some ants protect herds of aphids against ladybirds. In return, the aphids provide them with honeydew, a nutritious sugary liquid the sap-sucking aphids produce. The ants 'milk' the aphids by caressing them with their antennae.

GLOSSARY

ADAPTATION Changes in a plant or animal that increase its ability to survive and reproduce in its particular environment.

AGGREGATION Flock or other collection of animals that group together to gather food, to mate, to migrate or for some other common purpose.

AMPHIBIAN Member of the vertebrate class Amphibia, which lives both on land and in water. The class is divided into three main groups: those without tails (frogs and toads); those with tails (salamanders and newts); and legless creatures called caecilians.

ANTENNA One of a pair of feelers (antennae) on the head of many insects, crustaceans and other invertebrates, such as centipedes and millipedes. Sometimes used for defence.

AQUATIC Describes an animal or plant that grows or lives in or near water.

ASEXUAL Describes an animal that reproduces without sexual activity (mating).

BALEEN Horny plates of a material called keratin which hang down from the upper jaw of toothless whales. Also called whalebone. The plates act like sieves to trap food from the water.

BIRD Member of the class Aves; they are warm-blooded, egg-laying vertebrates with two wings and two legs. Most are well-adapted for flight but some are flightless.

BROOD Offspring produced at one hatching or birth. Used mainly for the young of egg-laying animals.

BUDDING Method of asexual reproduction in simple organisms in which new individuals develop from outgrowths of cells (buds) on the parent.

CAMOUFLAGE Means by which animals blend into their surroundings or otherwise deceive predators and escape their attention.

CARNIVORE Any meat-eating animal. More specifically any member of the mammalian order Carnivora, which includes cats, bears, dogs and badgers.

CARRION Dead flesh; carrion-eaters live on dead animals rather than killing live prey.

CARTILAGE Tough, flexible material that makes up part, or all, of the skeleton in some animals, including rays, sharks and skate. Also called gristle; it is found in the human nose and ear-flaps.

CASTE A 'social class' amongst some social insects, such as termites. Different castes perform different tasks within the community.

CHRYSALIS See PUPA.

COLONY Group of animals that live close together. Colonial animals often consist of numerous individuals linked together. Among them are corals and some jellyfish.

COMPOUND EYES Eyes of insects and some crustaceans (such as crabs, shrimps and lobsters); they are made up of hundreds or even thousands of tiny lenses, each of which provides an image, giving the creature a wide area of vision.

CONCEPTION Moment of fusion of a female egg cell and a male sperm (fertilization) to form a new individual.

CROP Food storage compartment in the throat or stomach of birds and many invertebrates.

CRUSTACEAN Member of a group of hard-shelled, mainly aquatic animals, including crabs, shrimps, barnacles and woodlice.

DIMORPHISM Occurrence of two forms in one species; sexual dimorphism is the difference between males and females. Often the male is larger, stronger or more brightly coloured than the female.

DIURNAL Describes an animal that is active during daylight hours.

DOWN Soft, fluffy feathers of young birds or the fine layer of feathers that forms the main insulation of adult birds.

EMBRYO 1. Young plant still enclosed in its seed. 2. Developing animal still in its egg or, in mammals, at an early stage of development inside the mother's body.

EVOLUTION Process by which plants and animals gradually change over successive generations, resulting in better adaptation to the environment and eventually producing new species. The driving force of evolution is natural selection – the survival of the fittest.

FERTILIZATION Fusion of the sperm of a male animal and the egg of a female to produce a new individual.

FISH Cold-blooded, aquatic vertebrates with gills (for breathing) and fins. They belong to several classes. Some are bony, some are cartilaginous. Some live in the sea, some in freshwater, and some spend part of their lives in both.

GASTROPOD Member of a group of molluscs that includes snails and slugs, limpets and whelks. Most have a single, coiled shell with two pairs of head tentacles. They move by means of a muscular foot.

GESTATION In animals that give birth to live young, the period of pregnancy from conception to birth.

HAREM Permanent or temporary group of animals consisting of one breeding male and several females, each with her own young.

HATCHLING An animal that has recently hatched from an egg.

HERBIVORE An animal that feeds on plants.

HERMAPHRODITE An animal or plant that has both male and female reproductive organs.

HIERARCHY Among social animals, a 'pecking order' in which animals of higher status have the right, for example, to eat or mate ahead of animals of lower rank.

INCUBATION 1. Keeping eggs safe or warm until they hatch. 2. Period of time between laying and hatching of an egg.

INSECT Member of the class Insecta, a very large group of invertebrates; they have three pairs of legs, a pair of feelers and most also have two pairs of wings.

INVERTEBRATE Any animal without a backbone. About 90 per cent of all animal species are invertebrates.

ISOPTERA Order of insects that includes termites.

KERATIN Hard substance made of protein that forms nails, claws, hairs and feathers.

LARVA (plural larvae) Stage in the metamorphosis of certain animals, such as butterflies and frogs. Caterpillars and tadpoles are larvae.

LEK Territory used by males for the sole purpose of attracting females.

LEPIDOPTERA Butterflies and moths; they all have two pairs of scaly wings. Lepidoptera means scale-winged.

MAMMAL Any member of the class Mammalia. All are warm-blooded and most are hairy. The female feeds her young on milk from her body and most give birth to active, live young. Humans, monkeys, cats, mice and whales are all mammals.

MARINE Describes animals and plants that grow or live in or near the sea.

MARSUPIAL Mammals, such as kangaroos, opossums and koalas, which give birth to tiny young that continue to develop in a pouch on their mother's belly. The majority live in Australia, but there are some opossums in the Americas, too.

MATRIARCHY Group of female animals led by a dominant female. Males are allowed to enter the group only during the mating season. The females in a matriarchy care for and bring up their young together.

MEGAPODES Ground-dwelling birds, including the mallee fowl, that live in Australia and New Guinea. They rarely fly, and incubate their eggs in huge nests of rotting vegetation.

METAMORPHOSIS Process in which some animals change their shape completely during their lifetime. Frogs and butterflies are examples.

MIGRATION Regular movement of animals from one area to another and back again at certain times of the year.

MOLLUSC Any member of the phylum Mollusca; the name means soft, and most molluscs are soft-bodied – though many have shells. The group includes snails and slugs, octopuses and squid, and mussels.

MOULT To shed feathers, hair or skin.

NEONATE Newborn animal.

NOCTURNAL Describes animals that are active during the night.

NYMPH Young of an insect, such as a grasshopper or a dragonfly, which resembles a small adult without wings.

OMNIVORE Any animal that feeds on both plants and other animals. Most humans are omnivores.

ORTHOPTERA Order of insects that includes grasshoppers and crickets. The animals have large hind legs that enable them to leap. Desert locusts swarm and destroy crops.

OVIPOSITOR Egg-laying tube of most female insects. In some, it is hidden, in others it sticks out from the hind end of the body.

PARASITE Plant or animal that lives in or on another (the host), and feeds on it.

PHONATIONS Sounds which are pitched too high or low for humans, but which can be heard by whales.

PLANKTON Minute organisms that live on the surface of rivers, lakes and seas.

POPULATION DENSITY The number of plants or animals within a given territory.

PREDATOR A carnivorous animal that hunts and kills other animals (prey).

PREENING Grooming behaviour in birds of stroking their feathers to clean them, and sometimes to spread oil over them to make them waterproof.

POD Group of animals, such as seals and whales, that co-operate to catch food or protect their young.

PUPA (plural pupae) Stage in the metamorphosis of an insect between larva and adulthood. The pupa may move but it cannot feed. The pupa of a butterfly or moth is called a chrysalis.

REGURGITATE To bring up, for example, food stored in a bird's crop usually to feed its young.

REPTILE Any member of the class Reptilia; cold-blooded vertebrates with scaly skin. They include snakes and lizards, tortoises and crocodiles.

RUT Mating season of the deer, during which time males bellow and roar and frequently fight.

SIBLING Brother or sister.

SPAWN 1. Eggs of fish or frogs. 2. To lay large numbers of eggs in water.

SYMBIOSIS Close association between individuals of different species, from which both benefit.

SYRINX Vocal organ of a bird.

TERRITORY An area of land inhabited and defended by an animal or group of animals against others of the same species.

TRACHEA Part, or all, of the respiratory (breathing) system of many animals, including mammals and insects.

VELIGER Free-swimming larva of many molluscs.

VENOM Poison.

VERTEBRATE Animal with a backbone. Mammals, fish, birds, reptiles and amphibians are all vertebrates.

ZOOID An individual member of a colonial animal, such as a coral.

INDEX